LET'S MAKE ART

ART

WITH YOUR

HANDS
AND FEET

SUSIE BROOKS

PowerKiDS
press

Published in 2018 by **The Rosen Publishing Group, Inc.**
29 East 21st Street, New York, NY 10010

Cataloging-in-Publication Data
Names: Brooks, Susie.
Title: Art with your hands and feet / Susie Brooks.
Description: New York : PowerKids Press, 2018. | Series: Let's make art | Includes index.
Identifiers: ISBN 9781538323168 (pbk.) | ISBN 9781538322215 (library bound) |
    ISBN 9781538323175 (6 pack)
Subjects: LCSH: Handicraft--Juvenile literature.
Classification: LCC TT160.B76 2018 | DDC 745.5--dc23

Editor: Elizabeth Brent
Design: nicandlou

Manufactured in the United States of America
CPSIA Compliance Information: Batch BW18PK: For Further Information contact
Rosen Publishing, New York, New York at 1-800-237-9932.

CONTENTS

LET'S MAKE ART!

Look at the shapes of your hands and feet — what do they say to you? Can you see a bird, a fish, a dinosaur, or an airplane? If not, you will after reading this book!

WHAT YOU NEED

Making a handprint, footprint, or fingerprint is a fun way to start a picture. All you need are a few basic art supplies, plus your very own fingers and toes! Look in the recycling bin for old envelopes, paper bags, and cardboard that you can use as a background for your work. Scraps of wrapping paper, wallpaper, or magazine pages are great for extra bits of decoration.

FOR THE PROJECTS IN THIS BOOK, IT ALSO HELPS TO HAVE THE FOLLOWING MATERIALS:

- ✓ PAINT
- ✓ NEWSPAPER
- ✓ PAINTBRUSHES
- ✓ A SPONGE
- ✓ COLORED INK PADS
- ✓ A PENCIL AND ERASER
- ✓ SCISSORS
- ✓ GLUE
- ✓ PLAIN WHITE PAPER OR CARD STOCK
- ✓ COLORED PAPER OR CARD STOCK, INCLUDING BLACK
- ✓ COLORED PENCILS
- ✓ MARKERS
- ✓ YARN OR RIBBON
- ✓ BUBBLE WRAP
- ✓ A HOLE PUNCH

HANDY HINTS

BEFORE YOU START, LAY DOWN PLENTY OF NEWSPAPER TO PROTECT THE SURFACE YOU'RE WORKING ON.

KEEP A BOWL OF WATER, A CLOTH, AND A TOWEL NEARBY TO CLEAN YOUR HANDS AND FEET AS YOU WORK. PAPER TOWEL IS USEFUL FOR WIPING, TOO.

IT CAN TAKE A FEW TRIES TO MAKE A PERFECT PRINT. TRY THESE TIPS:
- COVER THE UNDERSIDE OF YOUR HAND OR FOOT EVENLY WITH PAINT (A SPONGE IS USEFUL FOR DOING THIS)
- PRESS YOUR HAND OR FOOT FIRMLY DOWN ON THE PAPER AND KEEP IT STILL TO AVOID SMUDGING
- LIFT YOUR HAND OR FOOT STRAIGHT UP AGAIN AFTERWARDS, HOLDING DOWN THE PAPER WITH YOUR OTHER HAND.

SOMETIMES PAINTED PAPER WRINKLES AS IT DRIES. DON'T WORRY — YOU CAN FLATTEN IT LATER UNDER A PILE OF BOOKS.

ALWAYS WAIT FOR YOUR PRINT TO DRY BEFORE PAINTING OR GLUING ON DETAILS.

WHEN YOU SEE THIS LOGO, YOU MIGHT WANT TO ASK AN ADULT TO HELP.

BLUE ZOO

You can make a whole zoo of friendly animals out of your handprints — even using just one color!

ELEPHANT

1 Make a handprint with your fingers and thumb spread out. The thumb makes the elephant's trunk.

2 Paint on ears, a tail, an eye, a mouth, and a pink cheek.

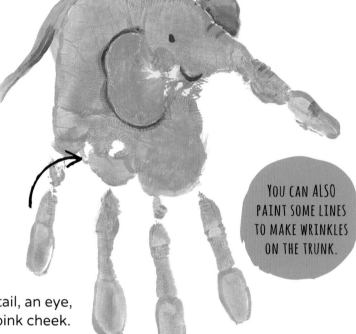

You can ALSO paint some lines to make wrinkles on the trunk.

HIPPO

1 Make another handprint, as above. Turn the end of the thumb into the hippo's head.

2 Paint on eyes, nostrils, cheeks, and a tail.

You could add some water and reeds, too.

6

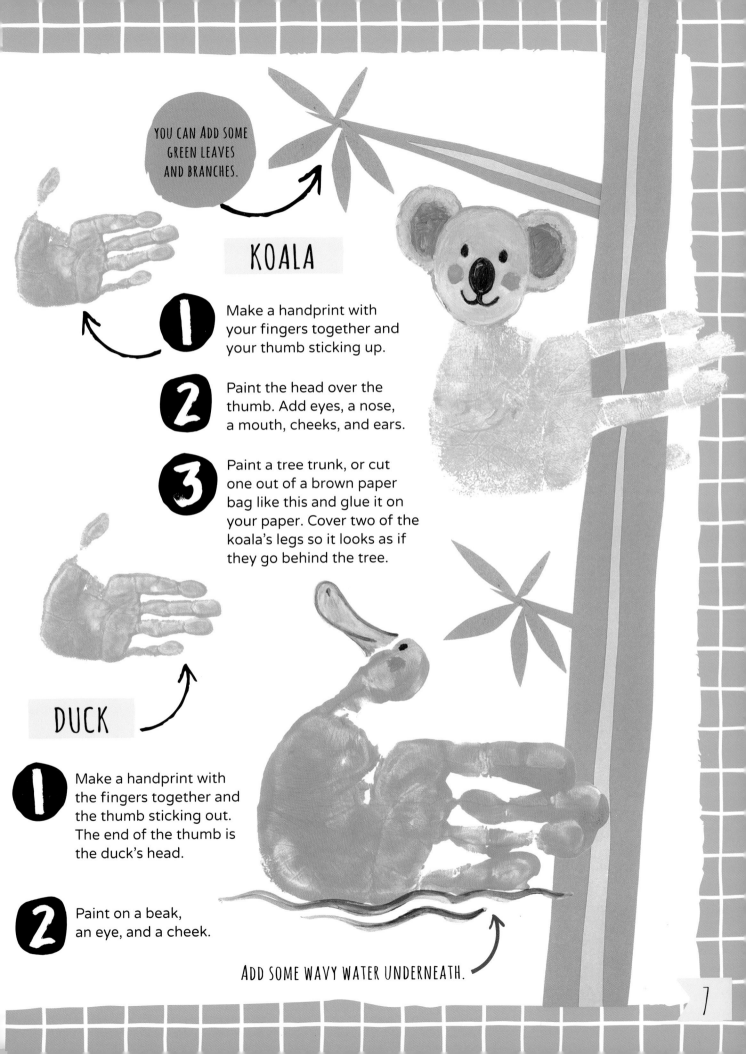

YOU CAN ADD SOME GREEN LEAVES AND BRANCHES.

KOALA

1 Make a handprint with your fingers together and your thumb sticking up.

2 Paint the head over the thumb. Add eyes, a nose, a mouth, cheeks, and ears.

3 Paint a tree trunk, or cut one out of a brown paper bag like this and glue it on your paper. Cover two of the koala's legs so it looks as if they go behind the tree.

DUCK

1 Make a handprint with the fingers together and the thumb sticking out. The end of the thumb is the duck's head.

2 Paint on a beak, an eye, and a cheek.

ADD SOME WAVY WATER UNDERNEATH.

PLAYFUL PENGUINS

USE THESE FUN FOOTPRINT PENGUINS TO MAKE A PICTURE OR EVEN A CARD!

1
Make a black footprint on a piece of card stock or paper and let it dry.

2
Use a paintbrush to paint two black wings. Paint two white dots for eyes. Cut a triangle from orange paper and glue it on for a beak.

USE A SPONGE TO PAINT ON A WHITE BELLY.

3
You can make a handprint into a sledding penguin. Keep your fingers and thumb together when you print.

PAINT ON A HEAD AND ADD A BEAK AND EYES AS ABOVE.

THIS SLOPE IS CUT FROM BLUE PAPER, WITH WHITE PAINT DABBED ON IT USING A SPONGE.

DRAW A SMILEY LINE ON THE BEAK.

USE BOTH FEET TO MAKE A PAIR OF SKIPPING PENGUINS!

HERE'S SOMETHING ELSE YOU CAN TRY.

Draw around your hand on white paper. Cut it out and glue it onto blue card stock. Now turn each finger into a penguin on an ice block.

PAINT THE BODIES AND GLUE ON ORANGE BEAKS AND FEET.

POLKA DOT DELIGHTS

You can make lots of pretty patterns with fingerprint polka dots! For gift tags or decorations, do this on small pieces of card stock. Use a cloth or paper towel to wipe your finger when you change colors.

PROJECT 1 Start with the middle dot, then surround it with circles of dots in a different color. Add as many circles as you like.

To make a dot, dip the tip of your finger in paint and dab it lightly onto paper.

PROJECT 2 For this pattern, start with the middle dot, then add more dots to make a square shape, like this one.

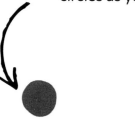

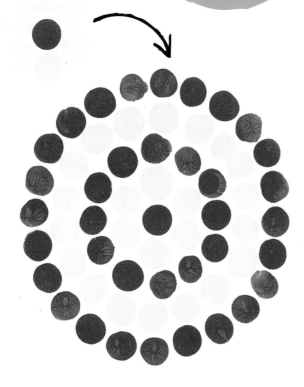

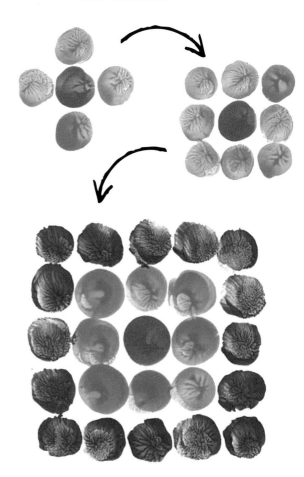

Start with a line of dots, then turn it into a cross. Fill in L-shapes in the corners until you have a complete square.

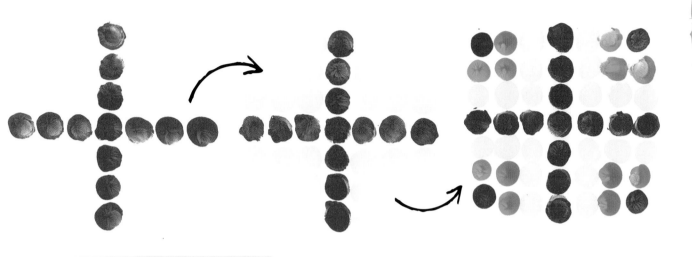

To make a gift tag, cut out your polka dot pattern. Make a hole near one edge using a hole punch. String through some yarn or ribbon and knot the ends.

TIP
You could glue your pattern onto colored card stock.

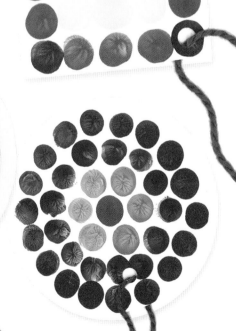

PROUD PEACOCK

Turn a hand stencil into a beautiful bird picture!

1 Draw around your hand on thin cardboard. Cut it out, keeping the outside part whole. This outside part is your stencil.

2 Lay the stencil onto white paper. Use a sponge to dab light-blue paint over the hand shape.

Cut out a yellow paper triangle to make a beak.

Draw on the eye, head, feathers, and legs.

3 When the paint is dry, lay the stencil back onto the paper so the fingers of the stencil are between the fingers of the blue hand. Dab dark blue paint into the stencil fingers.

4 Dip your finger in the dark blue paint and use it to paint the peacock's body.

5 For the tail tips, make lots of green and yellow thumbprints on a piece of white paper. Add fingerprint dots in a different color on top.

Cut out the tail tips and glue them to your peacock.

You could ALSO try a sideways peacock, like this one!

FACES IN A CROWD

You can have fun with thumbprint faces!
Colored ink pads and markers work well for this.

 Make a row of thumbprints and try drawing on faces like these:

HAPPY

CONFUSED

SURPRISED

SAD

 Practice drawing different hairstyles and expressions.

A ROUND MOUTH FOR A YAWN.

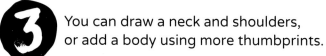 You can draw a neck and shoulders, or add a body using more thumbprints.

THESE PEOPLE ARE LOOKING OVER A FINGERPRINT WALL.

THERE'S A CAT UP A TREE.

4 Make a collection of faces in a crowd scene.

ARE SOME PEOPLE IN A HURRY? WHERE ARE THEY GOING? THINK UP A STORY TO GO WITH YOUR SCENE!

FAST FEET

Turn your footprints into speedy vehicles!
You can use the templates on p. 30 to help you.

RACING CAR

1 Make a colored footprint and let it dry.

2 Cut out shapes for the wheels, spoiler, and driver's helmet.

3 On a scrap of white paper, make a thumbprint and draw on a face. Cut this out and glue it onto the helmet.

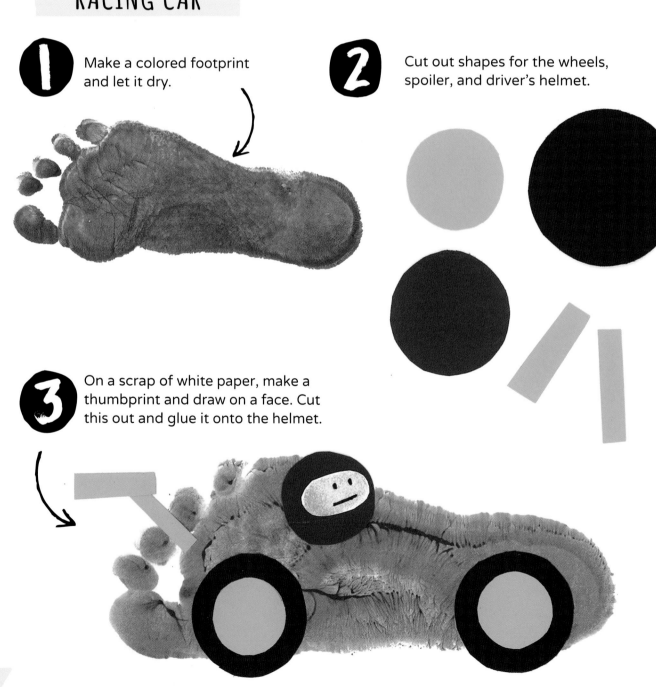

AIRPLANE

1 Make a colored footprint and leave it to dry.

2 Glue on colored paper shapes for the wings and tail.

3 Add some rows of windows – you could draw, paint, or fingerprint them on.

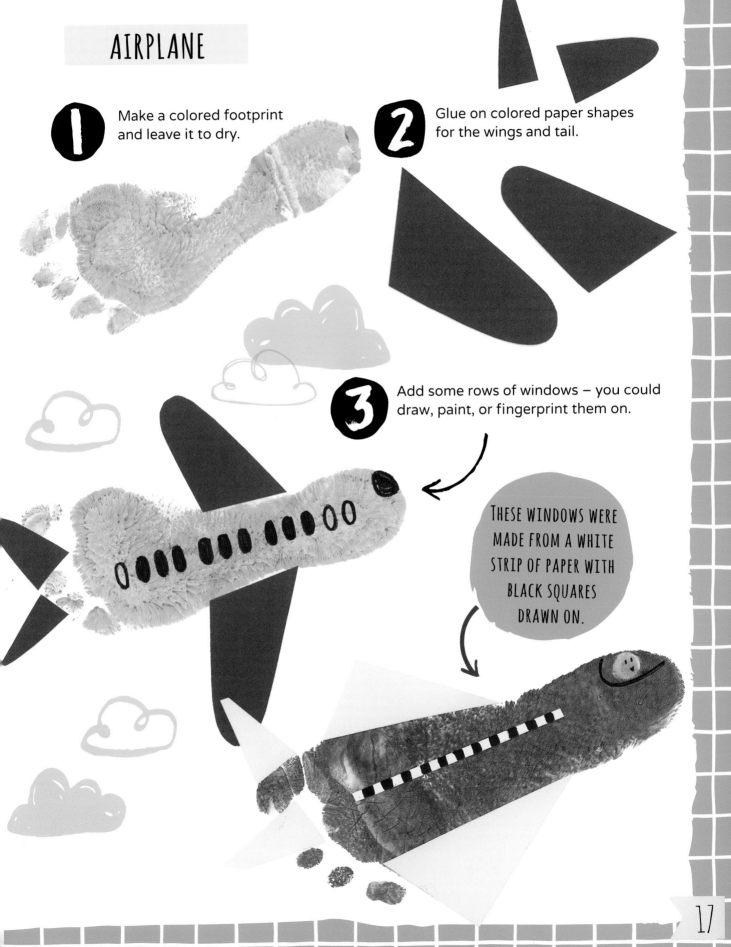

THESE WINDOWS WERE MADE FROM A WHITE STRIP OF PAPER WITH BLACK SQUARES DRAWN ON.

HANDY DINOSAURS

Make your hands into different shapes to create these awesome beasts!

TIP

For each dinosaur, draw around your hand on colored paper, as shown. Cut it out and glue it onto a paper background, then glue on the dinosaur features.

PROJECT 1

Draw and cut out a hand shape with the fingers and thumb spread out. Cut a separate tail shape and glue it on.

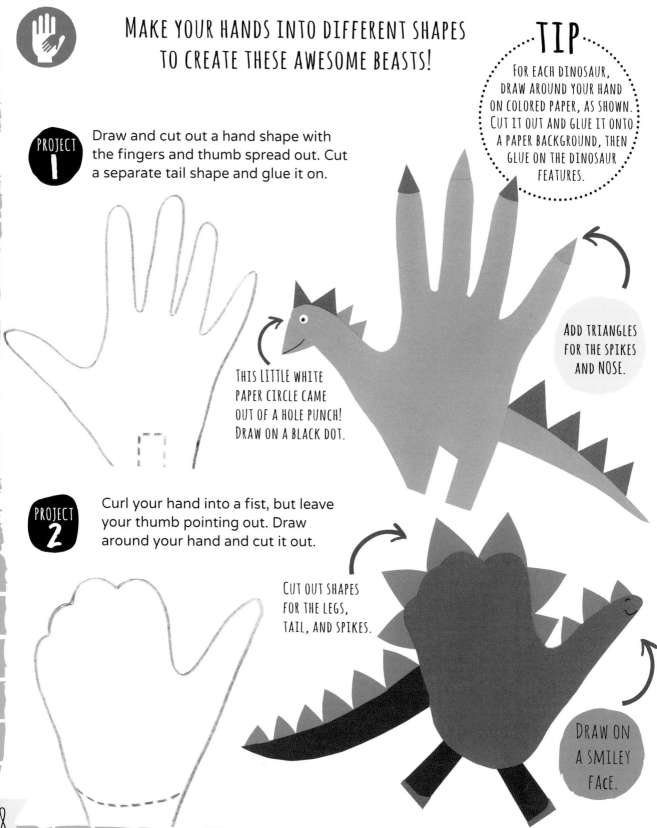

This little white paper circle came out of a hole punch! Draw on a black dot.

Add triangles for the spikes and nose.

PROJECT 2

Curl your hand into a fist, but leave your thumb pointing out. Draw around your hand and cut it out.

Cut out shapes for the legs, tail, and spikes.

Draw on a smiley face.

PROJECT 3

Rest your hand on its side with the fingers together and the thumb below them. When you've drawn around and cut out the shape, glue on paper circles and triangles for the eye, cheek, and teeth.

FINGERPRINT SOME DOTS ON THE DINOSAUR.

PROJECT 4

Draw and cut out a flat hand shape, then turn it upside down and trim it straight across the top. Cut out shapes for the neck frill, horns, and tail.

PROJECT 5

To make a plant like this, draw around a flat hand on corrugated paper and cut off the finger section. Snip some pink paper to make the flowers and glue them to each fingertip.

19

FINGERPRINT CANDY SHOP

YOU CAN MAKE A WHOLE CANDY SHOP OF TASTY TREATS USING JUST COLORED INK PADS, PENCILS, AND PAPER.

1 Start by drawing the outline of a jar.

2 Press your fingertip onto a brightly colored ink pad and print lots of dots inside the jar. Do one color, then wipe your finger clean and print another color.

THESE CANDIES ARE MADE FROM THUMBPRINTS. DRAW ON THE WRAPPERS AFTERWARDS.

3 For a lollipop, make two thumbprints in a heart shape, or fingerprint some dots in a circle. Draw on the sticks and an outline if you like.

4 You can turn lots of dots into a cupcake or a sundae! There are some templates on p. 31 to help with the bases.

Why not make a whole range of sweet treats and cut them out to display in your own candy shop?

Use colored paper for the background and glue on long, thin strips in a different color for shelves.

TRY MAKING DIFFERENT LIDS FOR YOUR JARS. YOU CAN DRAW THEM OR CUT THEM OUT FROM SCRAP PAPER.

TRY CUTTING OUT A CUPCAKE CASE FROM OLD WRAPPING PAPER, LIKE THIS.

BEES AND BUGS

TURN YOUR FINGERPRINTS AND THUMBPRINTS INTO A COLLECTION OF CUTE CREEPY-CRAWLIES!

BUMBLE BEE

1 Make a yellow thumbprint. Add two white wings using the tip of your index finger.

THIS BUTTERFLY IS MADE FROM FOUR THUMBPRINTS, WITH A PAINTED BODY AND MARKINGS.

2 When the paint has dried, draw on the details with a black marker.

SPIDER

1 Paint white dots on a dark thumbprint, then draw black dots for the eyes.

LADYBUG

1 Make a red thumbprint and let it dry.

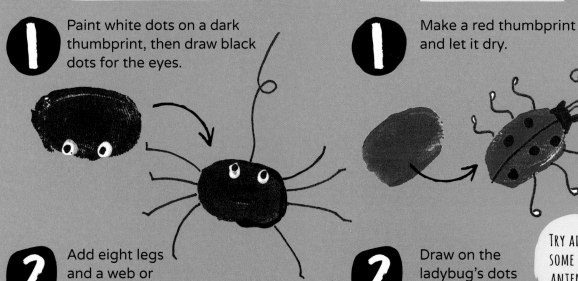

2 Add eight legs and a web or dangly thread!

2 Draw on the ladybug's dots and six legs.

TRY ADDING SOME CURLY ANTENNAE.

22

THUMBPRINT A SWARM OF BEES BUZZING TO AND FROM THE HONEYCOMB!

To make a honeycomb like this, cut a shape out of bubble wrap. Cover the bubbly side with paint, then press it onto the paper.

FLOWERS

1 Make a green thumbprint, then paint a stalk with a paintbrush. Let the paint dry before printing a clump of white dots with your fingertip.

HAUNTED HANDS

MAKE THESE SPOOKY GHOSTS WITH WHITE PAINT ON BLACK CARD STOCK AND PIN THEM UP TO HAUNT YOUR HOUSE FOR HALLOWEEN.

Make a white handprint and let it dry. Use black paint or a marker to add a scary face.

A WHITE FOOTPRINT CAN BE SPOOKY TOO.

FOR THIS SKELETON, MAKE A FIST WITH YOUR THUMB TUCKED IN, AND DIP YOUR BENT FINGERS INTO THE PAINT. MAKE A PRINT, THEN PAINT ON A SKULL AND SOME ARMS.

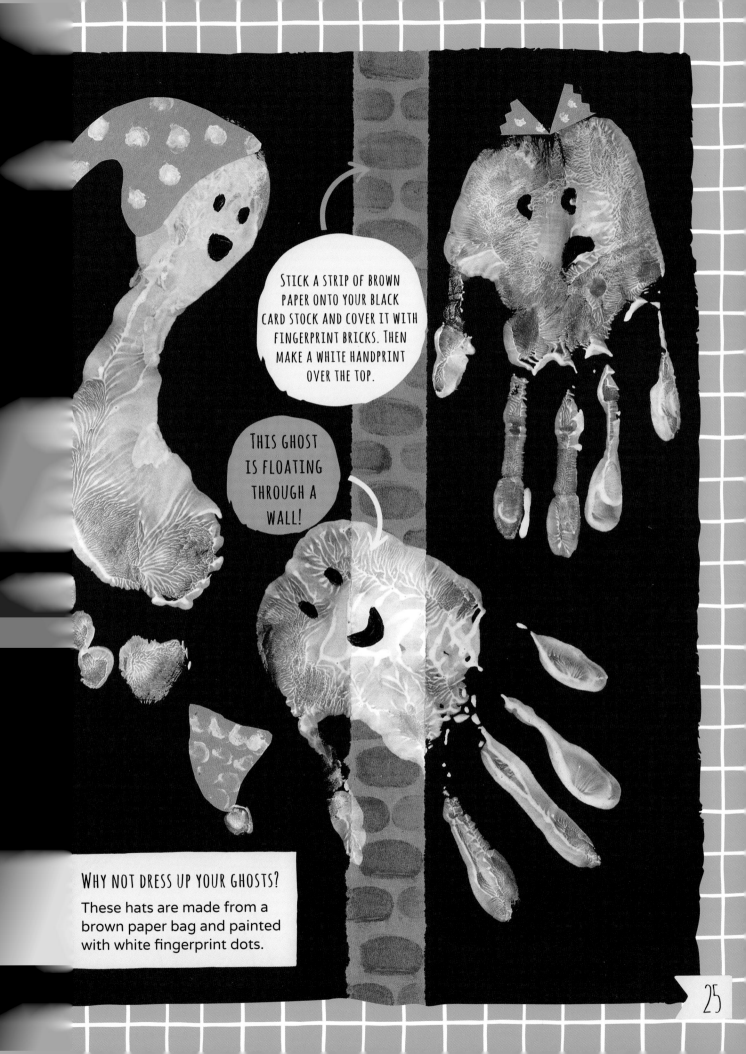

Stick a strip of brown paper onto your black card stock and cover it with fingerprint bricks. Then make a white handprint over the top.

This ghost is floating through a wall!

Why not dress up your ghosts?

These hats are made from a brown paper bag and painted with white fingerprint dots.

THUMBPRINT CIRCUS

COLORED INK PADS ARE USEFUL FOR MAKING THESE LIVELY CIRCUS CHARACTERS.

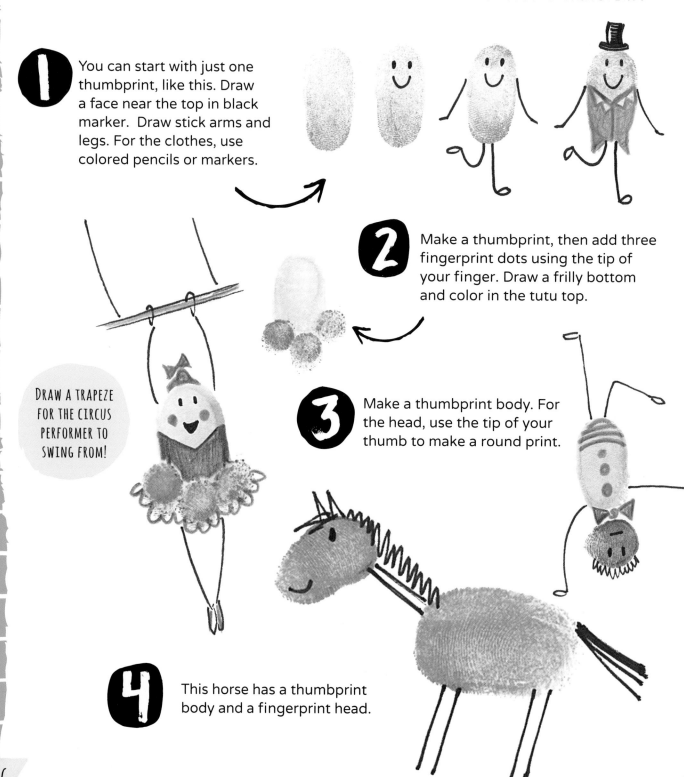

1 You can start with just one thumbprint, like this. Draw a face near the top in black marker. Draw stick arms and legs. For the clothes, use colored pencils or markers.

2 Make a thumbprint, then add three fingerprint dots using the tip of your finger. Draw a frilly bottom and color in the tutu top.

DRAW A TRAPEZE FOR THE CIRCUS PERFORMER TO SWING FROM!

3 Make a thumbprint body. For the head, use the tip of your thumb to make a round print.

4 This horse has a thumbprint body and a fingerprint head.

USE YOUR
FINGERTIP TO
PRINT SOME
BALLOONS!

YOU COULD
ADD SOME FACES
IN THE CROWD.

5 Try making a whole circus scene! Print the performers first, then paint or color in a yellow circus ring and some tent stripes around them.

FIST-PRINT FISH

USE YOUR FIST TO MAKE A WHOLE SHOAL OF THESE FANTASTIC FISH.

1 Hold your fist with your palm facing downwards and your thumb tucked in, and dip your bent fingers into some paint. Press your fist onto white paper.

2 When the paint is dry, draw the outline of a fish around it. There are templates on p. 31 if you need.

DRAW ON AN EYE AND A MOUTH.

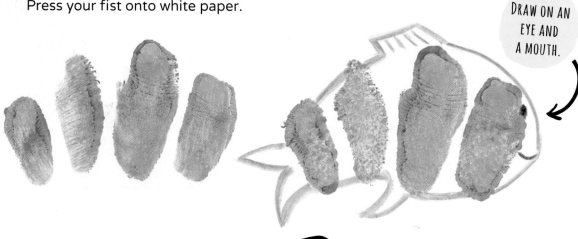

3 For this fish, add another color! Print a yellow fist and let it dry. Then clean your hand, dip it in pink paint, and print a fist over the top in the gaps.

4 For this fish, print one fist above another.

MAKE THE TAIL AND BOTTOM FIN FROM THUMBPRINTS.

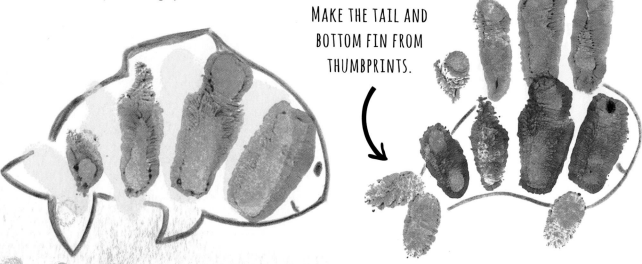

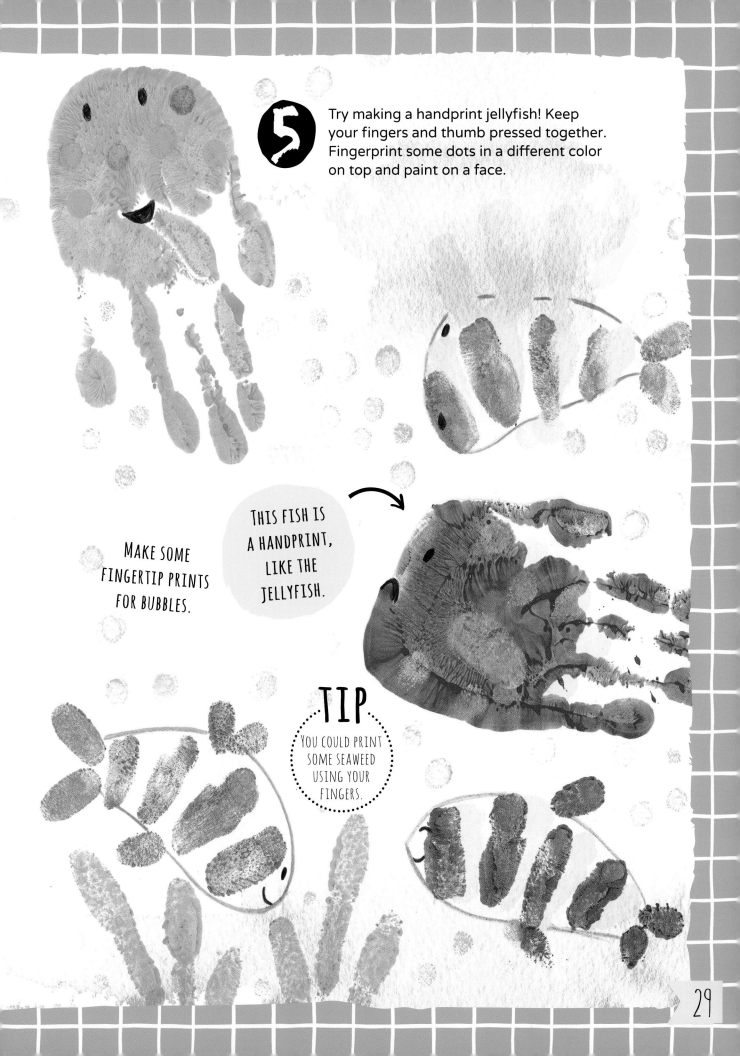

5 Try making a handprint jellyfish! Keep your fingers and thumb pressed together. Fingerprint some dots in a different color on top and paint on a face.

MAKE SOME FINGERTIP PRINTS FOR BUBBLES.

THIS FISH IS A HANDPRINT, LIKE THE JELLYFISH.

TIP

You could print some seaweed using your fingers.

TEMPLATES

FAST FEET
P. 16–17

FINGERPRINT
CANDY SHOP
P. 20–21

FIST-PRINT FISH
P. 28–29

FIST-PRINT FISH
P. 28–29

FINGERPRINT
CANDY SHOP
P. 20–21

FINGERPRINT
CANDY SHOP
P. 20–21

GLOSSARY

COLLAGE: ART MADE BY GLUING BITS OF PAPER, FABRIC, OR OTHER MATERIALS ONTO A SURFACE

CORRUGATED: RIDGED, LIKE THE INSIDE LAYER OF SOME CARDBOARD

INDEX FINGER: THE FINGER NEXT TO YOUR THUMB

OUTLINE: A LINE SHOWING THE SHAPE OF AN OBJECT

PRINT: AN IMAGE MADE BY PRESSING A PAINTED OR INKED OBJECT ONTO PAPER, CARD STOCK, OR ANOTHER SURFACE.

STENCIL: A THIN PIECE OF CARDBOARD (OR OTHER MATERIAL) WITH A SHAPE CUT OUT OF IT

TEMPLATE: A SHAPE USED AS A GUIDELINE TO TRACE